ROTTEN!

ROTTEN!

Vultures, BEETLES, SLIME,

and Nature's Other Decomposers

by Anita Sanchez

Illustrated by Gilbert Ford

Houghton Mifflin Harcourt
Boston   New York

To Gerald Durrell, and the anteater. —A.S.
To future scientists everywhere. —G.F.

Text copyright © 2019 by Anita Sanchez
Illustrations copyright © 2019 by Gilbert Ford

hmhco.com

The text of this book is set in Egyptienne and Regula.

Library of Congress Cataloging-in-Publication Data

Names: Sanchez, Anita, 1956– author. | Ford, Gilbert, illustrator.
Title: Rotten! : vultures, beetles, slime, and nature's other decomposers / by
Anita Sanchez ; illustrated by Gilbert Ford.
Description: Boston : Houghton Mifflin Harcourt, [2018] | Audience: Age 7–10.
| Audience: K to Grade 3. | Includes bibliographical references and index.
Identifiers: LCCN 2017061510 (print) | LCCN 2018002435 (ebook) |
ISBN 9781328534804 (eBook) | ISBN 9781328841650 (hardcover)
Subjects: LCSH: Biodegradation—Juvenile literature.
Classification: LCC QH530.5 (ebook) | LCC QH530.5 .S26 2018 (print) |
DDC 581.7/14—dc23
LC record available at https://lccn.loc.gov/2017061510

Manufactured in China
SCP 10 9 8 7 6 5 4 3 2 1
4500735975

Contents

IT'S A
ROTTEN WORLD

Plug your nose! Run for the hills!
Something smells . . . rotten.

Rot is everywhere! Not just in Dumpsters or faraway landfills. Decomposition is happening now in your backyard, your house—even between your teeth. Things decompose right under our noses, from the yogurt fermenting in the fridge to the food inside our bodies.

But wait a minute. Revolting as it seems, rot isn't necessarily bad. What would happen if nothing ever decomposed? What if every dried leaf, pile of dog poop, or dead animal just sat there forever and didn't rot away? Our cities would be piled high with garbage, forests would be clogged with logs, the ocean would be full of dead fish. Think about it . . .

Decomposition is part of nature. Decomposing seems like the last stop on the food chain—a dead end. But nature doesn't move in a straight line; it turns in a circle. After decomposition comes new life.

What Is Decomposition, Anyway?

Everything in the world—a beetle, a tree, a whale—is made of atoms of elements, such as carbon, oxygen, and nitrogen. Think of a jigsaw puzzle made up of billions of pieces, tiny and complex, perfectly fitting into one another.

But what do you do with the puzzle when it's finished? You have to take it apart to use the pieces again.

Decomposition is the process of breaking something down into its pieces. And as the bug, tree, or whale decomposes, all the uncountable billions of atoms that made up its structure are freed, ready to create new patterns.

Let's follow a single atom of nitrogen in the soil of a meadow. One sunny day, the nitrogen is absorbed by a root and becomes part of a blade of grass. A deer bites the grass, swallows, and down goes the nitrogen into the deer's stomach. The nitrogen becomes part of the deer's body.

After a hard winter, the deer dies. Its body decomposes, rotting away into the dirt. It's sad, smelly—and yucky! But the nitrogen atom sinks back into the soil. In spring it's sucked up by a root. The fresh green grass is eaten by a hungry fawn, and nature's cycle starts again.

Exploring Rotten

Decomposition isn't always ugly and disgusting. And, believe it or not, it isn't always smelly. So unplug your nose! Get ready to take a trip into the world of rotten. Sometimes it's a gross journey—but not always.

Like new grass springing from the remains of a dead animal, decomposition can seem almost . . . magical.

CHAPTER ONE

DUNG BEETLES

Rolling Rotten

I n a shadowy Egyptian tomb, a priest bends over
the mummy of a Pharaoh, chanting magic spells
as he winds linen strips around the body. Among the
strips, he places amulets shaped like lions or cobras, meant to
protect the king on his perilous journey to the afterlife. Directly
over the mummy's embalmed heart the priest places the most
powerful charm of all: a solid gold dung beetle.

* * *

Ancient Egyptians, even the most powerful kings and
queens, worshiped the miraculous power of dung beetles.
Egyptian artists created jewelry, paintings, and even
giant statues of these lowly insects, which they called
scarabs. They worshiped Khepri, a powerful god
shaped like a man with the head of a monster-size
dung beetle.

But why did they adore bugs that eat poop?

To the ancients, the scarab was a magical symbol of life triumphing over death. Dung beetles lay their eggs in a pile of manure, and when young beetles burst forth from a decomposing cow flop, it can seem like a miracle. Some dung beetles roll balls of dung across the ground, pushing with their hind legs. In Egypt, this symbolized the sun's magical journey through the heavens. Imagine a giant dung beetle rolling a blazing sun across the sky!

DUNG BEETLE ANTENNAE

How do dung beetles find all that smelly stuff? They don't have noses, but they do have antennae that are supersensitive to scents. The beetles wave their antennae in the air, pick up the tasty aroma, and fly toward it. They can get to a pile of dung seconds after it hits the ground!

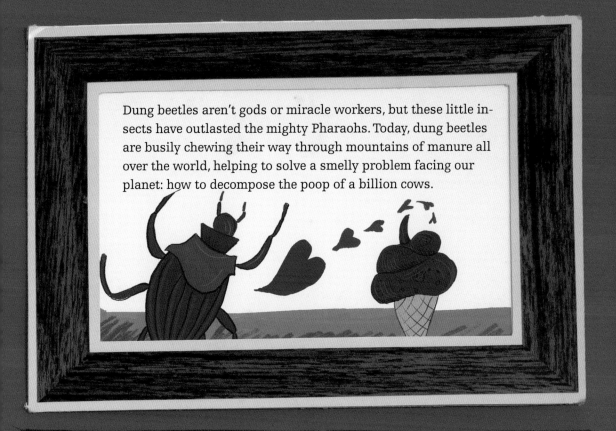

Dung beetles aren't gods or miracle workers, but these little insects have outlasted the mighty Pharaohs. Today, dung beetles are busily chewing their way through mountains of manure all over the world, helping to solve a smelly problem facing our planet: how to decompose the poop of a billion cows.

WHY DO SOME THINGS SMELL BAD TO US?

We're attracted by the luscious scent of food that's good for us: a ripe apple or a juicy steak. But we're disgusted by the smell of things that might hurt us. If you ate spoiled meat or got too close to dung that carried disease, you might get sick.

Our noses have evolved with a keen sense of smell to protect us from stomachaches—or worse. A bad smell warns humans: Stop! Be careful!

Why Do Dung Beetles Love Dung?

Dung beetles eat the droppings of other animals. They don't have noses like ours and aren't repulsed by stinky piles of poop. They especially love the dung of animals that eat plants. Because plants can be tough to digest, there's still lots of good nutrition left after a cow has finished lunch.

There are thousands of species of dung beetles, and they come in three kinds: dwellers, tunnelers, and rollers. Dwellers live inside the pile, eating their own house, so to speak. Tunnelers chew their way through the dung, build cozy burrows underneath, and eat their roof. Rollers shape the dung into a giant ball—well, giant to them—fifty times their own weight. Then, working together, male and female beetles start the ball rolling.

DWELLERS

Where are they going with their disgusting ball? They're rolling it to a safe spot to raise a family. But beware! Another dung beetle may try to steal the ball, and the males will fight fiercely to protect their treasure.

Dung beetles sometimes crawl on top of their ball and face the sun. More proof that dung beetles are sacred sun gods in disguise? Actually, the beetles are using the sun as a compass, to help them find their burrow.

TUNNELERS

The beetles bury the dung ball, and the female lays eggs in it. Most insects just lay eggs and fly away, never to see their children. But many dung beetle species take good care of the kids. Both Mom and Dad protect the eggs till they hatch. Then the larvae devour their tasty nest of dung.

There are dung beetles all over the world, eating all kinds of poop. Some chew on cow manure, but others go for the delicious droppings of buffalo, elephants, or horses.

ROLLERS

Give Me Air!

A cow lifts her tail. Out comes a nice wet mound of manure. But in the shadeless pasture, the hot sun bakes the cowpie, forming an almost airtight crust. Only tiny amounts of oxygen leak in.

Oxygen is the fuel of decomposition. Things rot faster when there's plenty of air around—it's called *aerobic* decomposition. Aerobic decomposition produces only a small amount of gases, and it's (almost) non-smelly.

But when things decompose without much oxygen, it's called *anaerobic* decomposition. It's a much slower—and stinkier—process. Anaerobic decomposition creates sulfur-based gases that smell terrible. That's why a plastic-lined garbage can stinks.

But an even worse problem is the gases that don't smell. *Methane* is an odorless gas, so you'd think it would be no problem. But methane is very good at absorbing heat from the sun. That makes it a major cause of global warming. The pollution that's causing climate change doesn't come only from cars and factories—a lot of it comes from cow poop!

You might think—oh, well, how much air pollution can a cow flop cause? But there are a lot of cows on the planet Earth—more than a billion of them! And each cow can poop fifteen times a day.
You do the math.

Beetles to the Rescue

But here come the dung beetles! They chew their way inside the cowpie, tunnel around, and grab bits to make their rolling balls. They stir up the dung like a cook stirring a boiling pot, letting in air and water.

A pile of dung vanishes as if by magic. Manure that is crawling with dung beetles decomposes in hours instead of months. It's aerobic decomposition going on, and so much less methane is produced, thanks to the beetles.

Studying Rotten

"One evening at dark, from an average cowpat, I counted two hundred and six dung beetles exiting in six minutes," says Dr. Pat Richardson, a biologist from the University of Texas who has spent years studying these industrious insects and their relationship with dung. "I could hear the activity in that cowpat (lots of snaps, crackles, pops)."

Dung beetle scientists get down on their hands and knees in the pasture and look closely at things most of us don't want to see. One painstaking researcher counted more than a thousand beetles chewing on a single pile of dung.

"They work for free and love their work," says Pat. (She's talking about the beetles.) "They slurp it, haul it, roll it, fight about it, and bury it," she explains. "They simply live, eat, sleep, and dream dung."

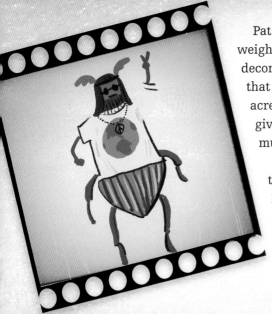

Pat and other scientists collect dung, weigh it, and clock how long it takes to decompose. On one Texas pasture she found that dung beetles buried a ton of poop per acre every day. Pastures with dung beetles give off smaller amounts of methane—as much as thirty percent less.

Dung beetles are major players in the battle against global warming. Maybe we'll never bow down before these bugs as gods—but perhaps the ancient Egyptians had a point when they worshiped the life-giving power of the mighty dung beetle.

Rot It Yourself:
THE SCOOP ON POOP

When you spot a nice, fresh pile of dog poop, hold your nose and take a closer look. Can you see any decomposers?

In warm weather, chances are a fly will discover the dog bomb before it cools off. Flies lay eggs in animal droppings, and soon hungry larvae (maggots) start feeding. Dung beetles don't prefer doggie dung, but ants, worms, and bacteria will flock to enjoy all those nutrients.

Butterflies love to land on poop. They slowly flap their beautiful wings as they feast on minerals in the droppings. Any kind of animal manure can be a gold mine of nutrients for decomposers.

CHAPTER TWO

SCAVENGERS

Eating Rotten

Look up! High overhead, a huge bird soars. Then another bird joins it, and another. Circling on rising currents of warm air, they weave graceful patterns, dancing in the air like ballerinas.

Suddenly one of the birds tilts its wings and glides earthward. Instantly, the others follow. They've caught the scent! The vultures are following their noses to a delicious dinner of rotten meat.

* * *

No doubt about it: a dead animal smells nasty. Most of us run the other way at the stink of a carcass rotting in the sun. But that powerful smell is like a dinner bell to a vulture. Because vultures are scavengers—animals that begin the process of decomposition by feeding on the flesh of dead animals.

WHY DOES A DEAD ANIMAL SMELL SO BAD?

Animal bodies are mostly made up of proteins. When proteins decompose, they break down into many types of molecules. Two of these, called cadaverine and putrescine, have incredibly powerful aromas—they smell horrible to humans but great to vultures! Plants have fewer proteins, so they don't stink as badly when they rot.

You'd think that eating a rotten carcass would make even a vulture sick. But vulture stomachs can cope with gunk that would kill most other creatures. Vultures can even digest meat that is covered with the *bacteria* of such deadly diseases as cholera, anthrax, or botulism. A mouthful of those germs could kill a human—but they're no big deal to a vulture. Powerful acids in the bird's stomach dissolve the bacteria. Vultures clean up the germs' breeding ground, and so help slow the spread of diseases.

Decomposer Selfie:
VULTURE NOSTRILS

Vultures have enormous nostrils, the better to detect the scent of rot. From high in the air a vulture can sniff out a dead rat hidden under a pile of leaves.

How to Eat Dead Stuff

Stomachs that dissolve deadly germs are a big help. And vultures have bizarrely bald heads, so they can sink their beaks into a tasty meal without getting bits of rotting flesh stuck to their feathers. Vulture beaks are sharp and hooked, so they can tear into tough hide. And since vultures are *diurnal* (active in daytime), their keen eyes also help them find their horrible food.

Still, vultures aren't the only creatures that eat rotten stuff. Many other creatures are scavengers, too. And when the vultures go to bed, the night shift gets busy.

Midnight Garbage Collectors

Clang, bang, clatter. The annoying sound of the trash collectors wakes you up. But wait a minute—it's the middle of the night! What kind of garbage collectors work at midnight?

Furry ones.

The enticing scent of rot wafts from a trash can with a loose lid. And once again that smell is a dinner bell. Raccoons, opossums, skunks—they all love a midnight snack. These small mammals are *omnivores,* which means they eat just about anything. Moldy crusts, stale chips, sour yogurt: bring it on!

If this diet makes the late-night scavengers seem disgusting, think of their habits as cleanup duty. In the Middle Ages, "scavenger" was just the official name for a person in charge of keeping the streets and public squares nice and tidy. True, it's annoying when unwanted guests make noise and leave a mess behind, but these nighttime prowlers clean up more messes than they create. Scavengers from coyotes to crows clean up many sad sights on our highways, finding good nutrition in the carcasses of road-killed animals.

Decomposer Selfie:
RACCOON FINGERS

Raccoon paws are like little hands with five agile fingers. Raccoons use them to open latches, pry the lids off trash cans, and unwrap all sorts of deliciously disgusting garbage bags.

Dead—or Alive?

There are thousands of species of scavengers, and a lot of them are very small! Blowflies lay eggs in *carrion*, the flesh of dead animals, and when the larvae hatch, they're surrounded by their favorite meal.

Flies love dead stuff, but they'll also lay eggs on a living body, even on humans. The eggs hatch into hordes of squirming larvae—the ultimate in gross! But actually the insects can be helpful. *Maggots* (fly larvae) eat only the rotten parts, leaving healthy flesh alone. Before modern disinfectants and antibiotics were discovered, healers would sometimes put maggots on people's wounds on purpose. The bugs decomposing the rotting, infected flesh might have saved a patient's life!

Dead Meals Don't Fight Back

Great white sharks. Killer whales. Grizzly bears. Even some of the biggest, baddest, most deadly creatures on Earth sometimes enjoy an easy lunch. Being a predator is just plain *hard work*. Stalking and capturing prey takes a huge amount of time and energy. And if the prey fights back, there's always the chance that the predator will be injured. Even a small wound to an eye or nose can be disastrous for a predator.

Great White Scavengers

Ever go swimming in the ocean and wonder if a shark is sneaking up on you? A bite from a great white is everyone's nightmare. The scent of blood in the water lures more sharks, lashing them into a feeding frenzy as they rip struggling prey apart. But what smells even better than blood? Rotting meat! Scientists studying shark behavior in the waters off South Africa happened to come upon the floating carcass of a dead whale. Dozens of sharks gathered to take advantage of the easy meal. And while biologists watched this picnic, they were surprised to see a whole new range of shark behaviors.

We don't think of sharks as being picky eaters, but when they are scavenging, they eat differently from when they feed on live prey. Sometimes the sharks would take a bite of bony, lean meat and then regurgitate it to take a piece of calorie-rich blubber instead. The researchers believe that the sharks were selecting the bits that were the most nutritious.

Sharks actually seem to prefer scavenging over hunting. While nibbling on the whale, sharks ignored the seals that were their usual prey. In another study, scientists observed sharks swimming past dozens of healthy sea turtles in order to snack on a nice, juicy dead turtle.

Decomposer Selfie:
SHARK TEETH

Shark teeth are razor-sharp and edged like a saw blade so that they can rip into the toughest whale hide. While sharks are scavenging, even a thick sea turtle shell is no problem for them.

Sharing Rotten

As sharks tear at the whale carcass, the immense body is slowly broken up into smaller and smaller pieces. Now other creatures, such as fish that could never bite through a whale's tough hide, can get a meal. Bits of leftovers float around for sea birds to grab.

Once the oily blubber is eaten, the whale's carcass sinks. Now it's dinner-time for a whole host of creatures that live lower down! A supernutritious food source is suddenly delivered to the ocean floor—like an unexpected pizza. Dozens of bottom-dwellers—crabs, fish, skates, rays, and snails—all get their share. Microscopic creatures floating in the water devour the specks of their leftovers. And so it goes, till every one of the uncountable trillions of atoms that made up the whale's body have provided food for something else.

Scavengers begin the process of decomposition, and from their banquet of death comes a wealth of new life.

CHAPTER THREE

FUNGUS

Slurping Rotten

They're lurking under your feet. They're floating through the air. They're hiding in the wilderness. They're sneaking inside your house. Wherever you go on planet Earth, you can be sure fungi aren't far away.

Mushrooms are just the parts we see—but there's a lot more to fungus than meets the eye!

* * *

What *is* fungus, anyway? For centuries, scientists weren't sure. It looks sort of like a plant, but it eats like an animal. Fungus can't make its own food from sunlight, air, and water the way green plants can. Just as animals do, fungus has to feed on other things—living or dead.

A fungus starts out as a *spore*, a speck so tiny it's almost invisible. Carried on the wind, spores can travel far from the parent fungus. If they land in the right place, they germinate, sending out slender rootlike threads. They grow into webs called *mycelia*, which look like tangles of whitish yarn.

Almost everywhere you walk, on grass, forest, or pavement, there's a dense web of mycelia beneath your feet. They wind their way through soil, reach deep into rotting logs, poke into dead animals. And all that fungus is *hungry*.

MYCELIA

How Does a Fungus Eat?

When you eat a crunchy pretzel or a tough piece of meat, it goes into your stomach, where acids and chemicals called *enzymes* soften and dissolve it so you can absorb its nutrition into your body. Fungi digest their food first, then eat it afterward. The mycelia ooze out powerful enzymes that can soften almost anything, even wood or bone. Once the meal is nice and mushy, the mycelia slurp up the nutrients.

Some fungi eat dead animals. Others prefer dead plants. Some are picky eaters—one type of fungus eats only pinecones, while a different species eats only pine needles. Some fungi eat other fungi.

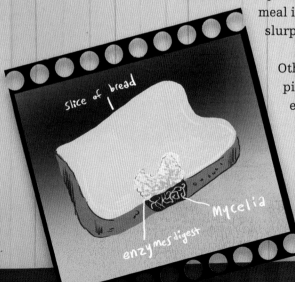

slice of bread

mycelia

enzymes digest

Decomposer Selfie:
CORPSE FINDER

Corpse-finder mycelia suck up the nutrition provided by a decomposing corpse. Then telltale clusters of mushrooms sprout over the spot where the body is buried. Sometimes they reveal the secret location of a buried murder victim!

Turkey Tails and Dead Men's Fingers

Tiny umbrellas. Gigantic horse hooves. Rainbow-striped bird's tails. There are more than a million kinds of fungus, in all shapes and sizes and colors. One kind—called "dead men's fingers"—looks weirdly like a human hand reaching out of the ground. And all these fungi are looking for a good meal.

Fungi excel
at breaking down
the tough bonds that hold
the molecules of wood together.
When fungus feeds on a rotting log,
it turns the dead wood into crumbly, dark soil
called *humus*, which is perfect for growing new trees.
But sometimes fungi snack on things we really, really
don't want them to eat.

Before chemical preservatives were invented, fungus slithered its sneaky strands into the damp timbers of wooden ships. The fungus weakened the wood so much that the ships often sank. "Train wrecker" fungi decomposed the wood of railroad ties and sent trains crashing off the tracks. "House wrecker" fungi can soften up the timbers of a house so that the walls collapse and the roof caves in!

But sometimes fungi's weird eating habits can be pretty helpful to us humans. Turns out that some fungi are fond of the strangest food of all: pollution.

A Feast of Poison

Who would want to snack on toxic chemicals, drink pesticide, or lick up an oil spill? Humans and other animals would die if they tried to eat such poisonous food—but fungus can handle it!

Paul Stamets is a *mycologist,* a scientist who studies fungus. A truck maintenance yard near his home became contaminated with spilled diesel fuel. Huge patches of soil were bare and lifeless, stinking of fuel oil. Scientists call such polluted areas "brownfields."

Paul knew that fuel oil is made of hydrogen and carbon atoms bonded together in much the same way as they are in trees, for petroleum is made of plants and animals that decomposed long ago. Could fungi break apart petroleum oil the same way they take wood apart?

Paul and some other scientists sprinkled a pile of diesel-contaminated soil with spores from oyster mushrooms. Another pile, the same size, wasn't treated with spores. Both were covered with a tarp. What would happen?

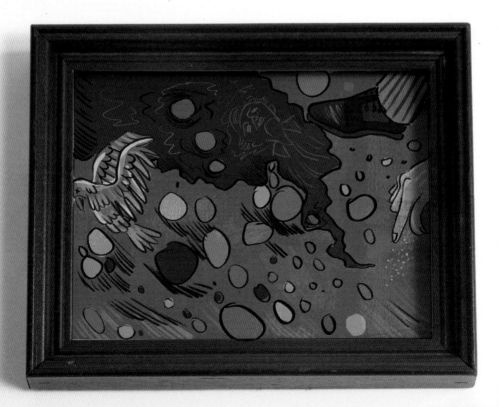

After four weeks the researchers returned. Paul pulled back the tarp over the fungus-treated pile. "Onlookers gasped in astonishment," he said. "We were greeted by a huge flush of oyster mushrooms, some more than twelve inches in diameter." The other pile was still black and foul-smelling.

Over the next month, insects fed on the mushrooms and then laid eggs. "Soon squirming larvae attracted birds, which brought seeds," Paul remembered, "and turned our pile into an oasis of life."

Now scientists are discovering other types of fungus that have a taste for oil spills, toxic chemicals, or cancer-causing pesticides. The challenge for the future is to figure out ways to put fungus to work cleaning up pollution on a large scale. Could fungus someday help cure the devastation caused by huge oil spills or chemical leaks? By using the power of fungus, Paul wrote, "brownfields can be reborn as greenfields."

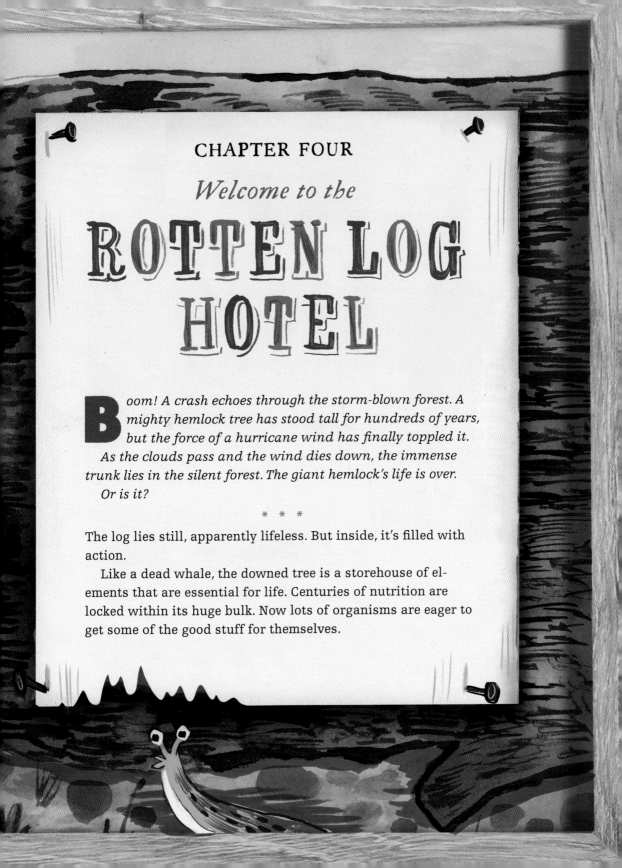

CHAPTER FOUR

Welcome to the

ROTTEN LOG HOTEL

Boom! A crash echoes through the storm-blown forest. A mighty hemlock tree has stood tall for hundreds of years, but the force of a hurricane wind has finally toppled it. As the clouds pass and the wind dies down, the immense trunk lies in the silent forest. The giant hemlock's life is over. Or is it?

* * *

The log lies still, apparently lifeless. But inside, it's filled with action.

Like a dead whale, the downed tree is a storehouse of elements that are essential for life. Centuries of nutrition are locked within its huge bulk. Now lots of organisms are eager to get some of the good stuff for themselves.

Like the whale, the tree's inner body is protected by a tough outer covering. A human would need an ax or a chain saw to cut into the tree. But sometimes bugs can work even better than chain saws.

Beetles chomp their way through the bark, leaving the trunk peppered with little round holes. And once the protective cover is open, here come hordes of even smaller invaders. Microscopic bacteria and fungus spores, often carried on the back of a munching beetle, enter the log through openings in the bark.

Ants and termites join in, crunching and munching on the inner wood.

The log becomes a giant hotel, with all sorts of visitors constantly checking in and out. Bacteria and beetles, slugs and snails and slime molds, millipedes and mice all find food and shelter in the log's holes and crevices. Carpenter ants build tunnels and roadways through the crumbling wood. Woodpeckers peck holes to reach the bounty of bugs. The dead tree is seething with life.

HOW COME WE'RE NOT INVITED?

Wood contains carbon, calcium, potassium, and other elements. Humans need these, too. We eat plants, such as corn, lettuce, and beans. Why can't we get nutrition from a log?

Imagine taking a bite of a tree. Even if your teeth could chew it into a mass of splinters that you could swallow (ouch!), your stomach couldn't digest it.

Wood is made of cells that have sturdy walls of fibers called cellulose and lignin. These make wood strong and dense—which is why an enormous tree's trunk can support all that weight. But human stomachs don't have the powerful enzymes that fungi ooze out, the ones that soften and digest the cells of wood. If you ate a bite of wood, it would just go in one end and out the other, with your stomach absorbing hardly any of the nutrients.

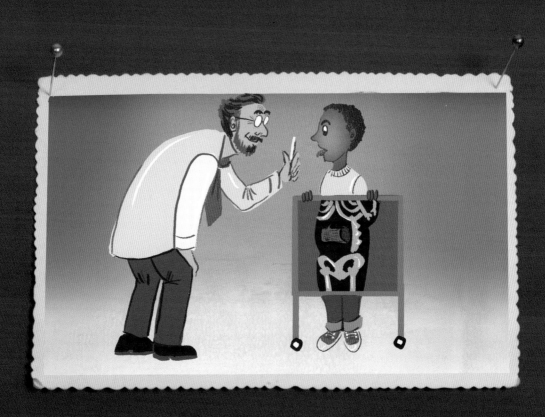

Smelling Rotten

To smell a tree decomposing, scratch and sniff the box below.

Scratch & Sniff

Don't smell anything? With all that decomposition going on, you'd think a huge rotting log would smell terrible. But it doesn't.

Garbage sealed in plastic bags doesn't get much oxygen or water, so it decomposes anaerobically—and remember, anaerobic decomposition is slow and very stinky. But a rotting log is surrounded by sunlight, rain-water, and lots of fresh air. The earthy fragrance of a forest is very different from the stink of a Dumpster.

Decomposer Selfie:
DOG VOMIT SLIME MOLD

It's slimy, shapeless, and moves very slowly. Weird, colorful blobs called slime molds often show up on rotting wood. They look like a mass of goo, but they're actually alive.

Slime molds are single-celled organisms that digest dead plants. They're not the same as fungus, but they're not plants or animals either. Scientists are still making new discoveries about exactly what they are and how these weird slimeballs eat, live, and reproduce.

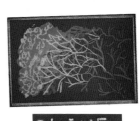

SLIME

Coffin to Cradle

The giant hemlock lies rotting away. Then one sunny morning a squirrel runs along the log, carrying his dinner—a seed-filled cone from a nearby hemlock. A seed drops onto the log.

The next day, the squirrel is back with another meal. He's a messy eater, and a few more seeds are scattered along the top of the log. And in the damp, rotten wood, some of the seeds begin to grow. Soon there's a line of little trees along the log, like babies clinging to their mother's back.

A log that nurtures the growth of new trees is called a *nurse log.* Like any good nurse, the log provides just the right care. The rotting wood has key elements such as nitrogen and potassium—just what hungry young trees need to grow strong! Sprouting on the nurse's back gives the babies a boost. Their high perch raises them above other plants that might block their sunlight. And the soft wood of the nurse log holds moisture like a sponge, giving the baby roots lots of water.

Years from now, a row of mighty trees will stand in a straight line. Hardly any trace of the old hemlock will remain—just a low hump in the earth, the ghostly outline of the fallen giant. The hemlock's death gives life to new generations: a future filled with trees.

CHAPTER FIVE

THE MIGHTY EARTHWORM

Moving Rotten

The great naturalist Charles Darwin enjoyed music, and sometimes he would take a break from his studies for a cozy family concert. Mrs. Darwin played the piano while son Frank played the bassoon. Five-year-old grandson Bernard tooted on a tin whistle.

But one afternoon the family orchestra tuned up their instruments for a very unusual audience. Mr. Darwin asked them to serenade a flowerpot full of slimy, wriggling earthworms!

* * *

Charles Darwin loved earthworms. He became famous for his books on evolution, but in his lifetime his bestseller had the following catchy title: *The Formation of Vegetable Mould, Through the Action of Worms, with Observations on Their Habits*. Darwin studied earthworms for years, measuring how they responded to light, heat, or even sounds. He finally discovered that worms literally change the earth through their mighty powers of decomposition.

The Mystery of the Sinking Rocks

Darwin got hooked on worms as a young man. His uncle showed him a pile of rocks that had been in the backyard for years and had sunk several inches into the soil. Darwin wondered: How could rocks sink?

Looking closely, he discovered earthworms wriggling underneath, and he suspected that the worms had something to do with it. But could an earthworm move a boulder?

Darwin searched for worms in gardens and farmers' fields. He prowled his backyard with a lantern to watch worms poke through the grass. He put earthworms in a flowerpot, studying how they reacted to the sounds of music and the vibrations of Mrs. Darwin's piano.

Finally he realized that worms were the solution to the rock mystery. Worms tunnel through the earth, up and down, endlessly stirring the soil as they feed. Slowly, over many years, even the biggest boulder is undermined and sinks into the soil.

But Darwin's discoveries led only to more questions: How do worms find food without eyes or a nose? And how do they eat without a mouth?

Decomposer Selfie:
EARTHWORM NOSES

Which end of a worm is which? Worms do have a front and a back. If you watch a worm, you'll see there's one end that moves forward. Earthworms don't have noses, but at the tip of their front end is a lobe of skin called a prostomium. *It's sensitive to touch, smell, and taste—part nose, part tongue. Worms suck food into a round opening at their front end, and this serves as a mouth.*

PROSTOMIUM

Eat Dirt!

If you put a worm in a box of sand, it would starve. Worms need organic material: bits of plants and animals that were once alive. As they eat, worms decompose the organic stuff in the soil, breaking it down into smaller pieces.

Tunneling underground, the worm devours the soil that's in front of it. Down it all goes through the long, thin tube of the worm's digestive system, till it gets to the gizzard, a tough-walled stomach. The bits of sand squeezed in the gizzard grind up the organic material. Worms have bacteria in their stomachs, enabling them to digest tough leaves and stems.

Worms absorb some of the soil's nutrients into their bodies. But all the rest comes out the back end in a long, thin strand of worm poop. (The polite word for it is *castings*.) Castings are packed with nutrients, broken down and ready to be absorbed by the roots of plants.

Rot It Yourself:

INVITE A WORM HOME

Ever think about getting a pet worm? "There is not a finer pet anywhere," says author and worm farmer Amy Stewart. "They are clean, quiet, and well-behaved." You can buy worms in a pet store or even order them online—look for red worms, which do well in worm bins.

Make your new pets a comfortable home in a large, shallow container. Put a few inches of shredded newspaper on the bottom, then add about six inches of sand mixed with soil. Add a small amount of food waste—a banana peel or a lettuce leaf—and put damp, shredded newspaper on top. Spritz the whole thing with water every now and then to keep the soil moist, but not soaking.

Then add worms, watch to see how long it takes them to decompose the food—and notice whether there are some treats your worms really like.

SIT   ROLL OVER   LAY DOWN

How Much Earth Can an Earthworm Move?

One worm can eat its own weight in *organic* material every day. (Imagine if humans did that!) A worm doesn't weigh much, true. But what if there are a lot of worms?

Darwin estimated that one acre (about the size of a football field) had fifty thousand worms.

But now scientists know that his estimate was way too low. A single acre of fertile farmland might contain *one million* worms.

Too Much of a Good Thing

Worms are superefficient at decomposing organic material. Sometimes they're a little too good.

Thousands of years ago, earthworms lived all across North America, but during the Ice Age, glaciers plowed the soil, obliterating many worm species. So some forests evolved without large species of earthworms.

When Europeans came to America, they often brought soil with them—as ballast for ships or in flowerpots—and sometimes there were stowaway worms inside. Earthworms are welcome decomposers in gardens and crop fields. But in the wilderness, too many non-native earthworms can damage forests—by decomposing too much. The worms churn the soil and eat so fast that they destroy the forest floor, chewing up the delicate layer of organic matter that sustains forest plants and animals.

If you go fishing and use worms for bait, don't dump them in a forest or by a woodland stream. Take them home and put them in your backyard.

Nature's Band-Aids

Humans can tunnel into soil, too—but we're not looking for dead leaves to eat. Humans dig for gold, coal, and other minerals. Mining causes massive damage to the land. So can construction or logging. When humans move too much soil around, the earth's protective layer of plants is stripped away. Once soil is exposed, it begins to erode; wind and water steal it speck by speck. Soon there's a wound on the earth, where nothing can grow.

Earthworms can help heal the wound, whether it's a huge abandoned coal mine or a small eroded corner of a playground. They tunnel through hard, compacted soil, letting air and water seep in. They decompose organic stuff in the dirt, then poop out castings full of the same nutrients you'd find in a bag of fertilizer. Seeds begin to germinate. As plants grow, their leaves provide more worm food, so more earthworms can move in.

But earthworms travel slowly. Centuries might pass before enough worms move into an area to make a difference. So biologists are studying the effects of "inoculating" eroded soil with a healthy dose of earthworms.

It's not a quick fix; repairing a damaged ecosystem takes time. But even a forest destroyed by logging or a mountainside devastated by mining can slowly recover if worms help out. Just as fungi can help clean up an oil spill, earthworms can heal the wounded earth using the power of rotten!

CHAPTER SIX

WHAT'S ROTTING

at Your House?

Okay, there's a lot of decomposition going on in forests, oceans, and even in your backyard. But there's nothing decomposing inside your house, is there? Couldn't be! Wait a minute. Open the refrigerator door and take a look . . . On the bottom shelf is a chunk of cheese . . . with a green streak of mold. Sniff the milk carton—smell a bit sour? Way in the back, an ancient doughnut is covered with white, powdery stuff—and it isn't sugar!

* * *

Just as fungi and bacteria decompose a log by feeding on it, they also chow down on stuff they find in your fridge.

Mold and mildew are types of fungus that can survive the chilly temperature inside the refrigerator. After food has been there awhile, spores germinate and mold begins digesting your leftovers. Sour milk is caused by bacteria feeding on the milk sugars.

Seems as if getting rid of the rot wouldn't be hard. Dump the milk and toss the mystery meat and moldy cheese! But there could still be rotten food inside your fridge. A lot of rot makes things taste bad, it's true. But just a little rot can taste delicious!

Hot fudge sundae, anyone?

SPORES

Good and Rotten

Does chocolate taste rotten? No way! But without decomposition, there would be no fudge, brownies, or chocolate chips.

Cacao beans are unpleasantly bitter —until they rot for a while. Letting cacao beans begin the process of decomposition allows them to develop a rich, complicated taste. Add sugar and fat, and you've got chocolate!

Does the thought of eating something rotten turn your stomach? Okay, let's use the word "fermented" instead. *Fermentation* harnesses the power of decomposition in order to change the taste of food.

Let It Rot . . . a Little

Before people invented cans and refrigerators, rot was a huge problem when it came to storing food. For thousands of years, hungry people have tried to slow down decomposition to keep food from rotting. People buried food in earthen jars or stone-lined pits. Months or even years later, the food would still be edible. And often the food—cabbage or corn, beans or breadfruit—had developed a tangy, sour flavor that tasted pretty good!

In Germany, fermented cabbage is sauerkraut; in Korea, it's kimchi. All over the world, people have rotted—oops, sorry, fermented—food in order to make it healthier, tastier, and longer-lasting.

You want to let the food rot a little—but not too much. Salt can slow down the rotting process because most food-spoiling bacteria won't grow in salty environments. That's why a lot of preserved food, such as bacon or corned beef, is salty.

Cucumbers taste okay—kind of bland. But let them decompose a bit, and they become a food most people love. Ferment the cukes in salt, and call them pickles.

Cheesemakers really have to know their decomposers—adding just the right fungi and bacteria to milk creates flavors of Cheddar, Swiss, Camembert, or mozzarella. Grapes will last for decades once fungi ferment them into wine.

But for thousands of years, no one understood the reason why fermentation worked.

Rot It Yourself:
YEASTY TREATS

Yeast is a type of fungus. Most bakers use Saccharomyces cerevisiae, *which means "sugar-eating fungus." Yeast spores are probably floating around in the air of your house right now. Or you can go to the store and buy yeast.*

Keep yeast in the fridge—cool temperatures keep yeasts alive but kind of slowed down and sleepy. Adding warm water wakes them up—and they wake up hungry! As they eat the sugars naturally found in flour, they give off a waste product—a gas called carbon dioxide. Bubbles of CO_2 make the dough puff up and rise. Look for the air holes caused by yeasts in any slice of bread.

Basic Bread Recipe

In a bowl combine:
3 cups whole-wheat flour
¾ cup warm water
1½ teaspoons salt

- Mix several billion yeast organisms (1 tsp.) in half a cup of warm water. (Not too hot!) Watch bubbles start to form as the yeasts get busy.

- Add the yeasty water to the flour mixture. Mix together—first with a spoon, then use your hands to knead the dough.

- Put dough in a bowl, cover with a cloth, and put in a warm place. In a few hours the dough should almost double in size.

- Squeeze the dough into a ball and let it rise again while the oven preheats to 350 degrees.

- Shape into small rolls, place on a cookie sheet, and bake for thirty minutes.

Invisible Decomposers

Bacteria are one-celled organisms, so small you need a microscope to see them. For most of human history, no one understood that these invisible creatures could cause disease, spoil food, and even kill people. But now we know that these specks of life are the most powerful decomposers of all.

Like all living things, bacteria need to eat. But they don't have mouths! They absorb food molecule by molecule through their cell walls. Like sharks breaking the dead whale into smaller pieces, bacteria break down what they feed on, bit by tiny bit. And like all living things, after they eat, they *excrete,* which means to get rid of waste products. Acids, carbon dioxide, and other chemicals seep out though the cell walls. Those waste chemicals are what change the taste and smell of food.

BACTERIA

Often the wastes that bacteria give off are acids. And that's good for humans. Why? Because most of the bacteria that cause food to spoil can't grow in acidic conditions. That's why fermenting a food makes it last longer: the good bacteria (a little rot) keep away the bad bacteria (a lot of rot).

There are millions of different species of bacteria, and they don't all eat the same things. Some bacteria eat sugars found in wheat or grapes or milk. Some bacteria eat cow manure. Some eat dead whales. Some eat dead trees. Some eat dead dung beetles. And some bacteria eat you.

BACTERIA

Your Own Personal Bacteria

They're crawling all over you right now.

You probably don't think of yourself as a habitat, but you generously provide food and shelter to billions of bacteria. They're on your hands, in your armpits, between your toes. They find shelter in your eyebrows and under your tongue. And they thrive inside your digestive system.

Ugh! Bacteria all over your body—that's bad, right? It's true that bacteria can cause all sorts of woes for humans. But don't panic! Fewer than one percent of bacteria species are *pathogens,* which cause disease. The bacteria on our bodies aren't making us sick.

They're just decomposing us, that's all.

No worries—these bacteria can be quite helpful. They feast on the stuff we don't need, such as dead skin cells, sweat, and skin oils. Bacteria prefer places that are damp and dark—they especially love armpits. When they eat your sweat, their waste products produce that "locker-room smell."

Welcome to the Food Chain

You're a link in the food chain every time you bite an apple or a hot dog. But as you chew, a little food might get stuck between your teeth. Bacteria that live in your mouth start feeding on the tasty morsel embedded between your molars, and they get some decomposition going right inside your mouth. The waste product of the bacteria's meal is a sulfur compound, which causes bad breath and cavities—so don't forget to floss!

After you chew, the food goes down into your stomach and intestines, where it's met by an army of bacteria. And most of them are helpful. Scientists call these "friendly" bacteria *probiotics*.

In your gut, acids and enzymes begin breaking food down into vitamins and nutrients. Probiotic bacteria help out, so your stomach has less work to do. And a mob of good bacteria can crowd out disease-causing bacteria.

Don't Kill Your Friends!

When you're sick, sometimes the doctor gives you an *antibiotic*. It can kill the nasty bacteria you don't want in your body, such as the ones that cause sore throats and earaches. But antibiotics also murder the friendly bacteria in your guts. That's why sometimes your stomach doesn't feel so great after you take an antibiotic. There's a delicious cure for this problem—eat some live bacteria! Get those good guys back inside you, helping your stomach do its messy job. To find live bacteria, just look inside your refrigerator. Billions of them are happily swimming in a tub of yogurt.

Eating Your Food Alive

If you find the words "live culture" on a container of yogurt, that means the bacteria in the yogurt are alive. Really.

Yogurt starts out as milk. Yogurt makers add just the right kinds of bacteria, called *lactobacilli*. As the bacteria decompose the milk, they release an acid that thickens the milk and gives yogurt that tangy taste.

In every spoonful of live-culture yogurt you put into your mouth, the living bacteria survive the trip through your digestive system and get to work helping your stomach do its best.

Decomposer Selfie:
MILK-LOVING BACTERIA

Lactobacilli acidophilus. *These creepy-looking critters are so small that billions of them fit in a teaspoon. They love to rot milk, and so they help create delicious cheese and yogurt.*

Eating Rotten

Eating rotten might not be so bad after all! Enjoy a pizza with crispy crust and extra cheese. Then try a corned beef sandwich made with sauerkraut, and pickles on the side. Finish with a hot fudge sundae. Savor the delicious taste of decomposition!

Got a stomachache now? A few spoonfuls of yogurt might help . . .

CHAPTER SEVEN

A Tale of

TWO SANDWICH CRUSTS

t's lunchtime on a bright spring day, and you're in the schoolyard, nibbling your peanut butter sandwich. On the way back to class, you toss the bread crusts into the trash—but one crust falls onto the playground grass. Next day, the dropped bread isn't there anymore. The trash can is empty. Both sandwich crusts are gone. But where?

* * *

First, let's follow the piece that fell on the ground. Even though the crust is half hidden in the grass, it can't hide from the sharp eyes of house sparrows. Like vultures spotting a deer carcass, the little dust-colored birds flock to the tasty morsel. Then they scatter as a shiny black crow zips down. He flaps away with a big chunk.

Breadcrumbs lie on the ground like snowflakes, but not for long. A small brown ant bumps into a crumb, as big as a boulder to him. The ant hurries to the anthill to spread the news. Soon dozens of ants are carrying their prize down into the nest to feed their larvae. Then fungi and bacteria move in to decompose any last specks.

Gone Away

But what about the other crust—the one that went into the trash?

At the end of the school day, the custodian's job is just beginning. She empties all the trash cans, pulling out each bulging plastic bag and tying it tightly. The trash bags are carted to the Dumpster, where they sit for several days.

In the hot Dumpster, decomposition begins. But there's very little oxygen in that squashed, airtight plastic bag. So it's anaerobic decomposition—the really smelly kind.

Then a huge garbage truck snorts and rumbles down the road. All the garbage is emptied into the back of the truck. Powerful mashers compact the bags so they'll take up less space. Most of the air is squeezed out.

Then the garbage truck roars off, taking the trash away.

But where?

There's No Such Place As "Away"

You'll never lay eyes on your sandwich crust again. But that doesn't mean it's vanished. The truck goes to your local dump and drops off its load. Plastic bags, one of them still holding your sandwich crust, tumble onto a huge pile. Eventually the mountain of garbage is squashed even more. Then it's dumped into a big hole called a landfill.

The landfill is lined with layers of waterproof clay and plastic to prevent germs and pollutants from leaking into the water table. When the pile is big enough, it's covered over with more clay and plastic.

And there the sandwich crust sits. For how long?

Digging Rotten

Would you eat a forty-year-old hot dog? Try some guacamole made decades ago? These tasty items and many more are waiting for you—in a landfill.

Dr. William Rathje called himself the world's first garbologist. He started out as an archaeologist, excavating Mayan temples and cities. Archaeology is the study of what humans leave behind, and Dr. Rathje knew that you could learn a lot about people by looking at what they throw away. He decided to excavate a modern landfill to see what was inside. And to his surprise, he found that landfills are packed with stuff that's *biodegradable.*

Biodegradable things can be broken down into their basic elements by nature's decomposing team—all those worms, fungi, bacteria, and bugs. Food waste, for instance, is easily biodegraded: potato peels, apple cores, or stale cookies will quickly decompose—if decomposers can get at them. Paper products such as cardboard boxes and newspapers are biodegradable, too. (After all, paper is made from trees.) Drop a paper towel in a forest and it will decompose in days.

But biodegradable things can't biodegrade when they're squished inside a landfill.

The Guacamole That Refused to Die

In waterproof, airtight landfills, Dr. Rathje found tons of decades-old newspapers, easily readable. He dug up enormous amounts of long-buried food that still looked almost good enough to eat: orange carrots, red lollipops, green lettuce. Then he unearthed a plastic tub of something creamy. "Hey!" Dr. Rathje shouted to his digging crew. "I think it's guacamole!" It was, still with chunks of bright green avocado. It sat next to a newspaper dated 1967.

In a landfill, there's almost no oxygen. No rainwater seeping in. No dung beetles to stir things up. No scavengers to break big things into small pieces. No earthworms to break down the little bits into littler bits. No way for fungus spores to get inside. Few bacteria.

So, almost no decomposition.

And what little decomposition goes on is anaerobic. Just as with the dried-out cow flops, decomposition happens very, very slowly, releasing massive amounts of dangerous methane into the atmosphere.

And then there are some kinds of garbage that seem as if they'll never decompose . . .

A Plastic World

Glance around the room you're sitting in right now. How many things are made from trees? Desks, tables, chairs, maybe. Your pencil. Paper is made from wood fiber, so your notebook comes from a tree. So does this book you're holding.

These things are made from organic materials, and just like dead trees, they're biodegradable. Someday they'll decompose, breaking down into carbon, nitrogen, oxygen, and many other nutrients that plants and animals can use again in nature's endless cycle.

But what about the rest of the stuff in this room? What's your pen made of? The rug, the computer screen, your phone? Toys, televisions, clothing; toothbrushes, shower curtains, soap dishes; cups, countertops, food wrap, sandwich bags: every year, in every room of the house, more and more of the things we use are made out of plastic.

What Is *Plastic?*

A century ago, there was no plastic on our planet. It's a substance made by people, invented in the early 1900s. Most plastics are made from fossil fuels such as petroleum—oil found in the earth that also gives us gas for cars and fuel for heating houses.

As soon as plastic was invented, people loved how handy it was, and they quickly found a million and one uses for it. Plastic is lightweight and can be molded into any shape. It comes in bright colors. It's cheap and easy to make. It's waterproof and tough, and it lasts a long time.

A really long time.

Drop a bread crust on the ground, and it's gone in hours. Drop a plastic toothbrush on the ground, and it could still be there in a hundred years.

Plastic is made up of long, complex strings of molecules linked together by humans in patterns very different from the way molecules are arranged in plants or animals. So decomposers don't recognize it as food. Earthworms and dung beetles ignore it. Vultures can't smell it.

Landfills are overflowing with plastic that's sitting there, not decomposing. But even worse is the plastic that doesn't make it into a landfill.

Killer Litter

Plastic is a deadly problem for animals that eat it or get stuck in it. Even the hardy insides of a goat can't decompose a plastic bag. Attracted to the bright colors of plastic litter, birds swallow plastic bottle caps. Sea turtles mistake floating plastic bags for jellyfish. Every year, thousands of animals eat plastic trash and die with their stomachs hopelessly blocked.

When plastic was created, no one knew how long it would take to decompose. Scientists now think that some kinds of plastic could take a million years to break down. But plastic has only been on the planet for less than a hundred years. We really don't know how long it will hang around.

Rot It Yourself:
A GARBAGE EXPERIMENT

Bury some garbage in a corner of the backyard. Choose different kinds—maybe a plastic water bottle, a paper cup, and an apple core. Wait four weeks, then dig up your buried treasure (don't forget to mark the spot!) to see what's decomposed

Plastic on the Menu

In 2008, Pria Anand was a college student on a very cool field trip. She and her biology classmates at Yale University traveled to the green, misty rainforests of Ecuador to collect fungi. Back in the lab, Pria and other students researched the fungi, hoping to find one that could break down the molecular bonds that hold plastic together. One day they noticed that the fungus specimen labeled *Pestalotiopsis microspora* had begun to nibble on a bit of plastic. Success!

Then, in 2016, a team of Japanese scientists made an equally startling discovery: bacteria that ate plastic! Where did these weird bacteria come from? Had these helpful little specks been around all the time, and no one had noticed them? Or have bacteria evolved to take advantage of a tasty new food source? No one knows. But the newly discovered bacteria, named *Ideonella sakaiensis*, think that plastic is fantastic.

There are still lots of problems to solve. The bacteria and fungi do what scientists want them to do in the lab, but how will they work outdoors? How can you persuade bacteria to eat plastic exactly where and when you want them to? What if plastic-eating fungi start eating the plastic in our homes or cars? As Dr. Ming Tien, a biochemist, points out, "It's a big leap to go from the test tube to the field."

Pria and a classmate, Jonathan Russell, are still working on finding ways to decompose plastic with living organisms. "Growing up in a world where pollution is going to be a big issue in the future, coming up with creative ways to tackle it gets me excited," Jonathan said. "I only hope that more people will take this on and get interested in it in the future."

Maybe you'll be the scientist who will find ways for decomposers to rot away our mountains of plastic garbage, turning it into healthy, living soil!

CHAPTER EIGHT

ROTTEN PEOPLE

I n a shadowy Egyptian tomb, an archaeologist bends over the mummy of a Pharaoh, carefully unwinding linen strips from around the body. He slowly unwraps the last bandage covering the head and gazes in awe at the face of a long-dead king.

The skin is brittle and blackened, but the eyes, nose, teeth, and hair are still there—after three thousand years.

* * *

Ancient Egyptians thought a lot about death—and life. They believed that a person's spirit would need its body in the afterworld, and so they went to great lengths to keep human bodies from decomposing. They understood how decomposition works, and they knew how to stop it—or at least how to slow things down. Mummies have lasted for millennia without rotting away. But how?

It's all about air and water. Things decompose quickly when oxygen and water are around. An autumn leaf on a damp forest floor will decompose in weeks. But if you want the leaf to last for years, press it in a book. The absorbent paper sucks the moisture away, and there's not much air between the pages. So, to make a mummy, remove water and air.

Ancient Egyptian embalmers began by removing all the wet stuff. Cuts in the veins let the blood drain out. They removed spongy organs such as kidneys, liver, and brains.

Then, just as though they were making pickles or bacon, they used salt to keep away bacteria and fungi. Embalmers crammed the hollowed-out body with salts and bug-repelling spices, wrapped it in bandages, and finally placed it in a sealed, airless coffin. Not much chance for worms, bacteria, or fungus spores to sneak inside! In the hot, dry climate of the Valley of the Kings, mummies had the perfect conditions to defy rot for an amazingly long time.

A Sweet Death

Humans have invented all sorts of ingenious ways to keep rot away from dead bodies. Maybe they got some ideas from the ways cooks kept food from rotting, using alcohol, sugar, or salt to fend off decomposers.

Honey is one of the world's most ancient treats, but it's also one of the world's oldest medicines. It's filled with chemicals that are especially good at fighting off hungry bacteria. Honey has been used for thousands of years to preserve fruits, vegetables, meat—and people. Embalmers in ancient China, Greece, and Arabia rubbed bodies with honey or beeswax. Sometimes the whole coffin was filled with honey, like a sticky bathtub for the corpse to float in.

Alexander the Great hoped to conquer the world, but he died unexpectedly in 323 B.C.E. at the age of thirty-two. His body was embalmed with perfumes, spices, and a sweet coating of honey. For centuries after his death, thousands of tourists—from peasants to emperors—visited his tomb and admired his handsome face.

Tapping the Admiral

In 1805 a British admiral named Lord Nelson was killed during the fierce sea battle of Trafalgar. His heartbroken crew wanted to take their victorious captain's body back to England for a glorious funeral. But how could he last on the long voyage home?

The ship's doctor had a bright idea—he placed Admiral Nelson's body in a barrel of brandy. There's a legend that some of the sailors "tapped" or drilled holes in the barrel to sneak sips, and to this day "tapping the admiral" means to have a drink on the sly.

Salt, sugar, alcohol, and spices—with their help, kings and heroes can defeat decomposition, but only for a while. Sooner or later the power of rotten breaks apart the molecules of every living thing.

Having Lee for Lunch

Lee Hays was a poet and folksinger, and he also loved to garden. He knew that to grow flowers and vegetables, you need fertile soil. He created a compost pile of weeds, grass clippings, and food scraps. He welcomed worms, beetles, and bacteria. Tendrils of fungus twined through the heap. And every now and then Lee stirred his beloved compost with a pitchfork to let in water and air.

Lee had diabetes, and even though he eventually lost both legs to the disease, he kept on gardening from his wheelchair. The rich humus of the compost pile nourished the plants he used to cook delicious food for family and friends.

When Lee Hays realized he did not have much longer to live, he made a decision. He knew that humans are made of the same kinds of molecules as ants, whales, or trees, and he saw no reason why he shouldn't end up the same way. A human body can nourish new life, just like a nurse log or a dead whale. "All that I am will feed the trees," he wrote, "and little fishes in the seas."

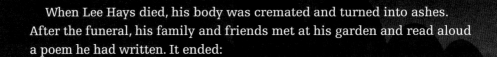

When Lee Hays died, his body was cremated and turned into ashes. After the funeral, his family and friends met at his garden and read aloud a poem he had written. It ended:

When corn and radishes you munch,
You may be having me for lunch.
Then excrete me with a grin,
Chortling, there goes Lee again!

Then they carefully mixed his ashes into the compost pile.

Rot It Yourself:
COMPOST PILE

You might not be ready to add yourself yet, but it's easy to create a compost pile. Make a heap of any sort of organic material—grass clippings, weeds, leaves, food scraps. Then sit back and let nature's decomposers do the rest.

You can help oxygen and water get into the pile by stirring it every now and then, but you don't have to. The stuff will decompose—just give it time. A three-foot-high pile in the fall will mostly decompose by spring, turning into a small heap of rich, dark humus, perfect for gardens and house plants.

The Beginning

Ocean or forest, desert or garden. High on a mountaintop or buried in a landfill. Deep in the wilderness, deep in the compost pile, or deep inside your stomach. Doesn't matter where on planet Earth you go—decomposition happens everywhere. It's nature's way of endlessly turning the old into new. Rotting isn't the end of the story, it's the beginning.

So when you smell that familiar odor, unplug your nose and breathe deep! The smell of rotten is the sweet scent of life.

Glossary

AEROBIC: in the presence of oxygen.

ANAEROBIC: without the presence of oxygen.

ANTIBIOTIC: a powerful medicine that kills bacteria.

BACTERIA: one-celled creatures, so small you need a microscope to see them.

BIODEGRADABLE: able to be decomposed by natural decomposers.

CARRION: the decaying flesh of dead animals.

CASTINGS: earthworm droppings.

DIURNAL: mostly active during the day and resting at night.

ENZYMES: chemicals produced by an organism, increasing the rate at which actions such as digestion occur.

EXCRETE: to get rid of waste products.

FERMENTATION: a process in which food is exposed to bacteria and fungi to change the taste and make food last longer.

HUMUS: the organic part of soil, formed by the decomposition of plants and animals.

MAGGOTS: legless insect larvae, usually of flies.

METHANE: an odorless gas produced by decomposition; a major cause of global warming.

MYCELIA: rootlike strands that are the growing form of fungi.

MYCOLOGIST: a scientist who studies fungi.

NURSE LOG: a decomposing log that nurtures the growth of new tree seedlings.

OMNIVORE: an animal that eats both plants and animals.

ORGANIC: any material that was once alive.

PATHOGEN: something that can cause disease.

PROBIOTICS: bacteria that are helpful to human digestion.

PROSTOMIUM: a noselike lobe of skin at the front end of an earthworm, sensitive to touch and smell.

SCAVENGER: an animal that feeds on dead or decaying organic matter.

SPORE: a reproductive cell produced by fungus and some plants.

Notes

10 *"One evening"*: Richardson, "Dung Beetles and Their Effects on Soil."
   "They work for free": Pat Richardson, quoted in Clark, "Dung Beetles Do a Job Nobody Wants."
28 *"Onlookers gasped"*: Stamets, *Mycelium Running*, p. 88.
40 *"There is not a finer"*: Stewart, *The Earth Moved*, p. 201.
63 *"I think it's guacamole"*: William Rathje, quoted in Corwin, "The Rotten Truth About Garbage."
69 *"It's a big leap"*: Ming Tien, quoted in McCrae, "Researchers: Fungus Can Break Down Plastics."
   "Growing up": Jonathan Russell, quoted in McCrae, ibid.
75 *"All that I am"*: Lee Hays, quoted in Courtney, "So Long to Lee Hays."

Bibliography

Browne, Janet. *Charles Darwin: The Power of Place*. Princeton, NJ: Princeton University Press, 2002.

Clark, Scott. "Dung Beetles Do a Job Nobody Wants." Dear Texas. April 6, 2014. (www.deartexas.com/dung-beetles-do-a-job-nobody-wants; accessed January 3, 2017.)

Corwin, Miles. "The Rotten Truth About Garbage." *Los Angeles Times*, July 17, 1993.

Courtney, Steve. "So Long to Lee Hays." *North Country News*, September 2, 1981.

Dyer, Betsey Dexter. *A Field Guide to Bacteria*. Ithaca, NY: Cornell University Press, 2003.

Fallows, Chris, Austin J. Gallagher, and Neil Hammerschlag. "White Sharks (Carcharodon carcharias) Scavenging on Whales and Its Potential Role in Further Shaping the Ecology of an Apex Predator." *PLOS One*. April 9, 2013. (www.journals.plos.org; accessed January 12, 2017.)

Featherstone, Alan W. "Decomposition and Decay." Trees for Life. 2015. (treesforlife.org.uk/forest/forest-ecology/decomposition-and-decay; accessed January 13, 2017.)

Fergus, Charles. *Trees of Pennsylvania and the Northeast*. Mechanicsburg, PA: Stackpole Books, 2002.

Frouz, Jan, ed. *Soil Biota and Ecosystem Development in Post Mining Sites*. Boca Raton, FL: CRC Press, 2014.

Grimes, William. "Seeking the Truth in Refuse." *New York Times*, August 12, 1992. (www.nytimes.com/1992/08/13/nyregion/seeking-the-truth-in-refuse.html?pagewanted=all&src=pm; accessed February 12, 2017.)

Humes, Edward. *Garbology: Our Dirty Love Affair with Trash*. New York: Avery Press, 2013.

LeBlanc, Cecile. "Tiny Earthworms' Big Impact." *Science News for Students*. Society for Science and the Public. October 28, 2016. (www.sciencenewsforstudents.org/article/tiny-earthworms-big-impact; accessed January 3, 2017.)

Lorch, Mark. "Scientists Just Discovered Plastic-Eating Bacteria That Can Break Down PET." ScienceAlert. March 10, 2016. (www.sciencealert.com/new-plastic-munching-bacteria-could-fuel-a-recycling-revolution; accessed February 4. 2017.)

McCrae, Kristen. "Researchers: Fungus Can Break Down Plastics." CNN. August 4, 2011. (www.cnn.com/2011/LIVING/08/04/fungus.eats.plastic; accessed March 1, 2017.)

Nuland, Sherman. *The Doctor's Plague: Germs, Childbed Fever, and the Strange Story of Ignac Semmelweis.* New York: W. W. Norton, 2003.

Pollan, Michael. *Cooked: A Natural History of Transformation.* New York: Penguin Books, 2013.

Quammen, David. *The Reluctant Mr. Darwin.* New York: W. W. Norton, 2006.

Rhodes, Chris. "Mycoremediation (Bioremediation with Fungi)—Growing Mushrooms to Clean the Earth." *Resilience.* July 6, 2014. (www.resilience.org/stories/2014-07-07/mycoremediation-bioremediation-with-fungi-growing-mushrooms-to-clean-the-earth-a-mini-review; accessed February 13, 2017.)

Richardson, Patricia, and Dick Richardson. "Dung Beetles and Their Effects on Soil." ManagingWholes.com. July 8, 2010. (managingwholes.com/dung-beetles.htm; accessed January 6, 2017.)

Roach, Mary. *Gulp: Adventures in the Alimentary Canal.* New York: W. W. Norton, 2013.

Russell, Jonathan R., Jeffrey Huang, Pria Anand, et al. "Biodegradation of Polyester Polyurethane by Endophytic Fungi." *Applied and Environmental Microbiology, American Society for Microbiology.* September 1, 2011. (aem.asm.org/content/77/17/6076.full; accessed February 14, 2017.)

Schaechter, Elio. *In the Company of Mushrooms: A Biologist's Tale.* Boston: Harvard University Press, 1997.

Slade, Eleanor M. "The Role of Dung Beetles in Reducing Greenhouse Gas Emissions from Cattle Farming." Nature.com. January 5, 2016. (www.nature.com/articles/srep18140; accessed January 3, 2017.)

Stamets, Paul. *Mycelium Running: How Mushrooms Can Help Save the World.* Berkeley, CA: Ten Speed Press, 2005.

Stewart, Amy. *The Earth Moved: On the Remarkable Achievements of Earthworms.* Chapel Hill, NC: Algonquin Books, 2003.

Tarlach, Gemma. "Rare Glimpses of Great White Sharks Scavenging Surprise Researchers." D-brief: *Discover* magazine, April 10, 2013. (blogs.discovermagazine.com/d-brief/2013/04/10/rare-glimpses-of-great-white-sharks-scavenging-surprise-researchers/#.WBO2S4WcHIW; accessed January 8. 2017.)

University of Miami, Rosenstiel School of Marine & Atmospheric Science. "Tiger Sharks Opt for Scavenging on Dead and Dying Sea Turtles as a Feeding Strategy: Study Provides New Insight into the Behavior of an Ocean Top Predator." *ScienceDaily,* August 8, 2016. (www.sciencedaily.com/releases/2016/08/160808115903.htm; accessed February 8, 2017.)

Vulinec, Kevina. "Most Parental Sharing of Brood Care." *The University of Florida Book of Insect Records,* Department of Entomology & Nematology | UF/IFAS. May 8, 1995. (entnemdept.ufl.edu/walker/ufbir/chapters/chapter_14.shtml; accessed February 9, 2017.)

Yoshida, Shosuke, et al. "A Bacterium That Degrades and Assimilates Poly(ethylene terephthalate)." *Science,* March 11, 2016. (science.sciencemag.org/content/351/6278/1196; accessed January 30, 2017.)

Index